Wider World

POWERED BY

Practice
Tests Plus

EXAM PRACTICE
CAMBRIDGE ENGLISH PRELIMINARY FOR SCHOOLS

Pearson Education Limited
Edinburgh Gate
Harlow
Essex CM20 2JE
and Associated Companies throughout the world.

First published 2016
Fourth impression 2017
ISBN: 978-1-292-10727-1

Set in Arial
Printed and bound in Great Britain by Ashford Colour Press Ltd

Photo acknowledgements
The publisher would like to thank the following for their kind permission
to reproduce their photographs:

(Key: b-botom; c-centre; l-left; r-right; t-top)
123RF.com: Joseasreyes 34tc, William Perugini 53c, 64t; **Alamy Images:**
Aflo Co. Ltd 14c, Age fotostock 34t, Image Source Plus 34c, Radius
Images 10b, YAY Media AS 52c, 64b; **Corbis:** Blend Images / Hill Street
Studios 13t, CI2 / Cavan Images 10tc; **Fotolia.com:** Cunaplus 16c, Oleg
Doroshin 40c; **Pearson Education Ltd:** Gareth Boden 10bc, 55c, 56c,
Studio 8 37t; **Shutterstock.com:** Tetra Images 34bc; **SuperStock:** Blend
Images 10c, 36l, Fancy Collection 10t, Socialstock 34b

Illustrations
Illustrated by Katerina Milusheva p. 23, 24, 25, 44, 45, 51, 54

All other images © Pearson Education

Contents

Exam Overview

The **Cambridge English: Preliminary for Schools** in English exam, also known as the **Preliminary Exam in English for Schools (PET for Schools)**, is an examination set at **B1 level** of the Common European Framework of Reference for Languages (CEFR). It is made up of **three papers**, each testing a different area of ability in English: Reading and Writing, Listening, and Speaking. The Reading and Writing paper carries 50% of the final mark, and the Listening and Speaking papers each carry 25% of the marks.

Reading and Writing   1 hour 30 minutes

Listening   30 minutes (approximately)

Speaking   10–12 minutes (for each pair of candidates)

All the questions in the examination are task-based. The rubrics (instructions) are important in every paper, and should be read or listened to carefully. They set the context and give important information about the tasks. The Cambridge English: Preliminary for Schools examination has topics and content specifically aimed at the interests and experiences of school-age candidates.

There is a separate answer sheet for recording answers for the Reading and Writing paper. At the end of the Listening paper, time is given for the answers to be copied onto a separate answer sheet.

Paper	Format	Task focus
Reading and Writing: Reading 5 tasks 35 questions	**Part 1:** multiple choice. Candidates read five separate short texts and answer multiple-choice questions on each one, choosing from three options.	Reading real-world notices, signs, postcards and other short texts for the main message.
	Part 2: matching. Candidates read and match five descriptions of people to eight short texts.	Reading several texts for specific information and detailed comprehension.
	Part 3: true/false. Candidates read ten statements. They then read a longer factual text to decide whether each of the ten statements is correct or not.	Processing a factual text and scanning it for specific relevant information.
	Part 4: multiple choice. Candidates read a longer text and answer five multiple-choice questions, each with four options.	Reading a text for detailed comprehension, and understanding the attitude, opinion and purpose of the writer.
	Part 5: multiple-choice cloze. Candidates read a factual or narrative text with ten gaps. They choose the correct word to fill each gap from four options.	Understanding vocabulary and grammar in a short text.

Paper	Format	Task focus
Reading and Writing: Writing 3 tasks	**Part 1:** sentence transformations. Candidates read five pairs of sentences linked in theme, and complete the second sentence in each pair so that it has the same meaning as the first sentence. They should not write more than three words.	Knowledge of vocabulary and understanding of grammatical sentence structure.
	Part 2: short communicative message. Candidates follow instructions given in the task and write a short communicative message. There are three points in the instructions candidates must include in their message. They should write 35–45 words.	Communicating three specific points in a short message, such as a postcard, note or email.
	Part 3: longer piece of continuous writing. Candidates choose to write either an informal letter or a story, using about 100 words.	Control and range of language in continuous text
Listening 4 tasks 25 questions	**Part 1:** multiple choice. Candidates listen to seven short monologues or dialogues and look at three pictures for each one. They choose the correct picture for each answer.	Listening to identify key information.
	Part 2: multiple choice. Candidates listen to a longer monologue or interview. There are six questions. Candidates choose the correct answer for each question from three options.	Listening to identify specific information and detailed meaning.
	Part 3: gap fill. Candidates read notes or sentences with six gaps. They listen to a longer monologue and fill in the missing information.	Listening to identify, understand and interpret information.
	Part 4: true/false. Candidates read six statements. They then listen to an informal dialogue and decide whether these statements are true or false.	Listening for detailed meaning, and to identify the attitudes and opinions of speakers.
Speaking 4 parts. Candidates take the test in pairs.	**Part 1:** examiner-led conversation. The examiner asks candidates short questions in turn for 2–3 minutes.	Giving factual and personal information.
	Part 2: simulated situation. Candidates are given a task to discuss together for 2–3 minutes, with visuals to help them.	Making and responding to suggestions, discussing alternatives and making recommendations. Candidates should negotiate with each other and make a decision.
	Part 3: individual extended turn. Each student is given a photograph to describe. They speak alone for about 1 minute, and the part takes 2–3 minutes.	Describing photographs using appropriate vocabulary, and organising an extended turn.
	Part 4: general conversation. Candidates talk to each other for about 3 minutes. The examiner gives them a task to discuss that is linked in theme to the pictures they described in Part 3.	Expressing opinions, likes/dislikes, preferences , experiences, etc.

Practice Test 1 with Guidance

Reading: Parts 1–5

About the paper

The *Reading and Writing* paper lasts for 1 hour and 30 minutes. There are five reading parts and three writing parts.

The Reading section includes a range of text types (for example, signs and notices, magazines, emails, texts, websites and brochures) and types of question. It tests your knowledge of vocabulary and grammar, and your ability to read and understand a range of texts. There are 35 questions in total and each question is worth one mark.

In the Writing section, you will write a variety of text types from sentences to longer continuous writing. The first part tests your grammar and is worth one mark per question. The second and third parts both test extended writing; Part 2 is worth five marks and Part 3 carries fifteen marks.

Part 1
In Part 1, you read five short information-based texts (for example, signs, notices, emails), and answer a question about each one. There are three options for you to choose from.

Part 2
In Part 2, you read five short descriptions of people and a set of short texts on a topic (for example, information about books or museums). You have to match each person to the best text for them.

Part 3
In Part 3, there is one long factual text to read and ten questions. You have to decide whether each question is true or false. The questions follow the order of the text.

Part 4
In Part 4, there is one long text, which includes some attitude or opinion as well as facts. You have to answer five multiple-choice questions with four options to choose from. The questions follow the order of the text.

Part 5
In Part 5, you read a short text which has ten gaps. You complete each gap, choosing the word that fits best from four options.

How to do the paper

Part 1
- Read the instructions and look at the example.
- Read each text carefully. Think about where you might see it and why it was written. Try to think of another way to say the same thing.
- Read the three options (A–C) and decide which one has the same meaning as the text.
- If you're not sure which option is correct, cross out any options that are clearly wrong, and see which are left. If you are still not sure, you could guess.

Part 2
- Read the instructions and the title of the text to get an idea of the topic.
- Read through the five descriptions of people and underline key words about each one.
- Read each section of the main text quickly, and highlight information that matches the descriptions. Don't just look for the same words – look for different words or phrases that have the same meaning.
- Read each description of the people again and carefully check the highlighted texts to find the best match. The ideas in each description may be in more than one text, but only one text includes *all* of the things the person needs or wants.

Part 3
- You don't need to read the whole text first. The text contains information that you may not need in order to answer the questions, and may include vocabulary you don't know. You won't need to understand every word to answer the questions.
- Read the instructions and the title of the text to get an idea of the topic.
- Read through all the sentences and underline key words.
- Read the text quickly and highlight parts where the information you need can be found. Look for words and phrases that mean the same as the key words you underlined in the sentences. The sentences are always in the same order as the information in the text.
- Read each section of the text you highlighted carefully and decide whether the sentence is true or false.

Part 4
- Read the instructions and the title of the text to get an idea of the topic.
- Read the text quickly to understand what it's about and how it's organised.
- Read the questions without looking at the options (A–D), and underline key words.
- Questions 22–24 follow the order of the text. Find the part of the text where each question is answered and read it carefully, underlining key words and phrases.
- Try to answer the question without using the options. Then read the four options (A–D) and choose the one that is closest to your own answer. Look for the same meaning expressed in different ways.
- Check that the other options are clearly wrong. If you are still unsure, read the text again carefully and look for reasons why some of the options may be wrong.
- For questions 21 and 25, you have to think about the whole text. Try to answer these questions without looking at the options and then choose the best answer.

Part 5
- Read the instructions and the title of the text to get an idea of the topic.
- Read the whole text, ignoring the gaps, to get a general understanding.
- Read the text again. At each gap, stop and try to predict what the missing word might be.
- Look at the options (A–D) and decide which one fits the gap. Read the whole sentence to check the meaning of the missing word. Check the words before and after the gap, for example, some words can only be followed by one preposition.
- If you're not sure which word to choose, decide which options are clearly wrong, and then see which are left. If you're still not sure, you should guess.
- When you've finished, read the complete text again and check that it makes sense.

Questions 1–5

Look at the text in each question. What does it say?
Choose the correct letter **A**, **B** or **C**.
In the exam, you mark your answers **on a separate answer sheet**.

Example:

0

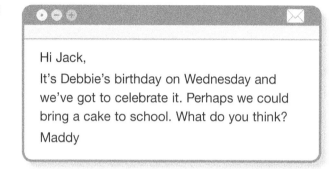

Hi Jack,

It's Debbie's birthday on Wednesday and we've got to celebrate it. Perhaps we could bring a cake to school. What do you think?

Maddy

Why has Maddy written the email

A To remind Jack about a birthday celebration.

B To ask Jack to buy something for the celebration.

C To suggest a way to celebrate.

| 0 | A ⊔ | B ⊔ | C ▬ |

1

Spanish Classes

- Mondays and Thursday 4.00 –
  beginner level

- Wednesday 4.30 –
  intermediates

Sign list by Friday.

A There are Spanish classes every day except Tuesday.

B You need to know some Spanish already to join a class.

C There is a time limit for showing you are interested.

2

*Annie,
I'll be home about 5.30 after a quick visit to supermarket, so don't worry about cooking.
Could you record Dad's favourite car programme at 5.15 on Channel 3?
Don't forget!
Mum*

What should Annie do?

A Start to prepare dinner.

B Do something for her father.

C Watch an interesting programme.

3

Dad,
I'm at the station. Miss Barker let us leave straight after the test so I got the 4.30 train. No problem if you can't pick me up right away. I can wait in the café.
Tilly

A Tilly has missed her dad at the station.

B Tilly is earlier than she'd thought.

C Tilly wants her dad to come and get her now.

4

Play guitar?
Want to join a rock band?

Come to our practice –
Wednesday evening, school hall.

A A school group is looking for a new member.

B There's a performance of rock music on Wednesday.

C Students can practise guitar playing on Wednesdays.

5

Hi Mike,
Did I leave my homework at your house – maybe on the table? Have a look and text me. I can call round after swimming if you're going to be in.
Beth

What does Beth want Mike to do?

A Help her with her homework later.

B Phone her after swimming.

C Check something for her.

Tip strip

Question 1: What types of classes are advertised? What must you do if you want to join the class?

Question 2: Underline the different actions in the note. Who will do them?

Question 3: Where is Tilly now? Why is she there? Is this usual or unusual? What does she suggest?

Question 4: What's happening on Wednesday? Who will be there? Who do they want to come?

Question 5: What is Beth's problem? What is she definitely going to do later? What's her suggestion?

Reading: Part 2

Questions 6–10

The teenagers below all want to buy a new book.
On the opposite page, there are descriptions of eight new books for young people.
Decide which book would be most suitable for the following teenagers.
For questions **6–10**, choose the correct letter (**A–H**).
In the exam, you mark your answers **on a separate answer sheet**.

6

Molly reads a lot of scary books, but she doesn't like them to be too unbelievable or too violent. She thinks it's scarier if you read about events that could possibly happen.

7

Luke is a bit of a romantic and likes a love element in the books he reads. That, combined with a story that moves really fast, is his ideal book.

8

Marty enjoys science and has a bookshelf full of factual science books. He wants a book to help him understand environmental problems.

9

Tommy likes anything that is exciting. He also enjoys travelling and likes finding out about places he's never been to.

10

Linzi is more interested in fact than fiction and she likes reading true-life stories about people. She's particularly interested in reading about how people's backgrounds affect their lives.

Tip strip

Question 6: What does Molly like and not like in a book? What makes a book good for her?

Question 7: There are two things that Luke likes in a book. What are they?

Question 8: What is Marty interested in? Does he like invented stories or things that are true? What doesn't he understand?

Question 10: Does Linzi prefer true or invented stories? Is she more interested in people or things?

New Books

A Turner Returns
If you love the great James Bond spy movies then you'll love the latest Jackson Turner – the charming teenage spy. There is a lot of action as Jackson chases a criminal mastermind across Europe. Of course, his new girlfriend Ella is never far from his side!

B Planet Future
Do we really want to know what is going to happen in our world? This book combines fact and fiction and creates a future world that is very possible and very frightening. Written by the team of thriller writer Les Down and scientist Al Weller, it's a book that will certainly make you think.

C Highway Terror
When Gabby and Dylan decided to spend their gap year in the USA they had no idea that a car journey was going to turn into a nightmare. Along the way they pass through several US states that we don't normally hear so much about. This book will keep you up all night!

D Barnes Saves the Day
People love a good mystery and this is definitely a good one. Young detective Torrie Barnes and his friend Amelia solve a problem that is confusing everyone! With a gadget that Tom, a keen scientist, has himself developed, they track a killer, but it will keep you guessing all the way!

E A Taste for Adventure
Most books that celebrities write about themselves can be a bit dull, but travel journalist Ed Summer's autobiography, which describes his childhood and teenage years in Scotland, is anything but boring. The stories explain why he developed into one of the best travel journalists in the world.

F Night Spirits
Books about vampires and spirits have become very popular in recent years and this new ghostly adventure by Susa Davis is one of the best. Lots of blood, howling and scary wolves. Not recommended for people who have problems sleeping!

G The World About Us
Are you confused by the theories scientists give us about global warming and climate change? A new book by Helena Verner puts it all in simple language anyone can understand. So, whether you're worried about the weather in Australia or volcanoes in Iceland, you can read about it here.

H Katy's Dog
The death of the lovely Labrador in *Marley and Me* made animal lovers everywhere burst into tears. Well, get the tissues ready again for another sad read. *Katy's Dog* tells the true story of a disabled girl and her wonderful guide dog. But it's funny, too, and very well-written.

Reading: Part 3

Questions 11–20

Look at the sentences below about an amateur dramatic club called LADS.
Read the text on the opposite page to decide if each sentence is correct or incorrect.
If it is correct, write **A**.
If it is not correct, write **B**.
In the exam, you mark your answers **on a separate answer sheet**.

---

11 Teenagers who join the society can enter an acting competition to win free lessons.

12 The trainer will be a well-known television actor.

13 LADS has won awards both inside and outside the UK.

14 Anton appeared in a film when he was very young.

15 As well as plays, it's possible to buy tickets to watch play readings, too.

16 Anyone in the society can recommend plays for a play reading.

17 Actors also need to learn technical theatre skills.

18 Young children will soon have their own technical and creative writing workshops.

19 There is more than one type of membership of LADS.

20 LADS encourages audiences to take part in their performances.

Tip strip

Question 11: Find and <u>underline</u> who exactly will get the lessons and what they need to do.

Question 12: Look for an adjective to describe the actor and some information about what he's done.

Question 13: Did *Kinder Transport* win the international competition? Read the whole sentence carefully.

Question 14: You need to read several sentences to find the answer. What happened to Anton?

Question 15: What does the text say about 'audience' in connection with the play readings?

Question 18: Check the tense in the statements and in the text.

Question 20: Think about the words 'during' and 'after' to get the right answer.

Join the LADS!

☆ ☆ ☆ ☆ ☆ ☆ ☆ ☆ ☆ ☆ ☆ ☆

Could you be the next Hollywood sensation? Or perhaps you'd like a role in your favourite TV soap! Your search for fame could start right here on your doorstep. The award-winning Lonsdale Amateur Dramatic Society is on the look-out for new members. The first ten teenagers to join before 1st October will be given a series of free acting lessons by local professional actor and star of the TV series *Chancellor*, Anton Markham.

Lonsdale Amateur Dramatic Society (or LADS as it is known locally) started sixty years ago and since then it has won local and national awards for some superb productions. *Kinder Transport* just missed out on a top prize last summer at EuroDram, an international student competition. Many of our young members go on to drama school and some have even worked in films. Anton was discovered in this way after joining our junior section when he was just eight years old. The director of the film *The Young Oliver* came with his father to see a production of *The Tempest*. The rest is, as they say, history!

As well as putting on shows every month, we also have regular play reading evenings. Members choose a new play or a play that they think others will enjoy and we read it together. This is a chance to find out about plays you don't know and also a great opportunity to meet other members and have a fun evening. There's no audience, there's no need to learn lines, so no pressure – and it is usually a really good laugh.

However, LADS is not only for acting hopefuls. We also give help and opportunities to young people who want to learn other theatre skills such as lighting, directing and even costume design. Our older, more experienced members advise newcomers and everyone can get practical experience in one of the many shows we put on. In the coming year, we also plan to run a series of workshops for under 11s who want to learn how to write short plays and design costumes and posters, etc.

If you lack the confidence to perform on a stage or prefer watching good plays to helping produce them, then why not become an associate member? For a small annual fee you can get a discount on tickets for our shows. You can also join discussion groups with our actors and directors after a show, and take advantage of cheap tickets for trips to London shows, too.

So, what are you waiting for? Click (**here**) for more information about how to join. And, young would-be actors – do it soon and get those lessons!

Questions 21–25

Read the text and questions below.
For each question, choose the correct letter **A**, **B**, **C** or **D**.
In the exam, you mark your answers **on a separate answer sheet**.

← →   🔍 [   ]

Trip to Science Museum

Jake Collins

The school trip to the robot exhibition at the Science Museum took place last Thursday and it was a very interesting experience. I personally don't usually enjoy looking round exhibitions, unless they are of pictures or photographs! I imagined this exhibition would be boring, but in fact I was proved wrong.

The trip was planned by Miss Matthews because our class is entering a national science competition in November to design and build a small robot. She thought the exhibition would focus our ideas. The exhibition, which is touring Europe, has come from the USA and consists of some amazing machines that have just been developed. There were a lot of complex robots to see and we didn't manage to look at all of them even though we were there for about four hours.

I was particularly impressed by a robot waiter that could take orders and serve food. We were allowed to test it and I ordered so many sandwiches that I couldn't eat my lunch! My friend Anna loved the robot pets that purred just like real cats and she played with them for ages. They even turned their heads in the direction of your voice.

As well as fun robots there were some films about large machines that they couldn't demonstrate in the museum, including a driverless tractor that did farm work all on its own. It's a little worrying that machines like these could replace the jobs of lots of real people.

Our class may not win the robot building competition, but the exhibition certainly gave us some good ideas. It continues until next Monday and I can certainly recommend a visit, even if you're not that keen on science!

Tip strip

Question 21: This question refers to the whole text. Read the text all the way through and then think about where you might see this and who will read it. Could it be in a newspaper, a magazine, on a school website? What sort of information does it give? This should help you choose.

Question 22: Think about where the exhibition came from and when the machines were made. Why was four hours too short?

Question 23: What did the writer and his friend do at the exhibition? What was the film about?

Question 24: Did the writer think his class might benefit from the visit? How?

Question 25: Look at the whole text again. Does the writer give his opinion about science? Does he want to return? What does he say about the film?

21 What is the writer's main purpose in writing the text?

   A To advertise a new exhibition at a science museum.
   B To point out the use of robots in our daily lives.
   C To report on a visit to a robot exhibition.
   D To encourage people to become interested in robotic science.

22 What does the writer say about the exhibits?

   A They were produced by European inventors.
   B They had won national competitions.
   C They were too complicated to understand in one visit.
   D They were recent inventions.

23 What could visitors do during the exhibition?

   A They could dress up and imitate the robots.
   B They could interact with the robots.
   C They could take pets round the exhibition.
   D They could watch a science fiction movie.

24 In the writer's opinion the exhibition

   A was inspirational for his class.
   B was going to finish too early.
   C was an opportunity to learn about different jobs.
   D was interesting for people who enjoy science.

25 What might the writer of the text say about the exhibition?

   A *I was impressed by some clever robots, but the visit hasn't changed my opinion about science.*

   B *I enjoyed the practical demonstrations, but I wish the food had been better.*

   C *I saw some interesting things which made me think about the future.*

   D *It was a better day than expected and I think I'll go back again next week for another visit.*

Questions 26–35

Read the text below and choose the correct word for each space.
For each question, choose the correct letter **A**, **B**, **C** or **D**.
In the exam, you mark your answers **on a separate answer sheet**.

Example:

0 **A** looking   **B** asking   **C** finding   **D** trying

0	A	B	C	D
	▬	▭	▭	▭

Who's for a Padel?

Are you **(0)** .... for a new game to play with your mates? Do you like tennis but **(26)** .... fed up chasing the ball **(27)** .... time someone hits it too far? Perhaps Padel Tennis is for you!

Tennis is a cool sport and it's a good way to **(28)** .... fit. However, **(29)** .... of us spend too long running after the ball. Padel Tennis was invented **(30)** .... Mexico in 1969 by Enrique Corcuera and it's now really **(31)** .... with players across the world. It is **(32)** .... to tennis, but the big advantage is that there are walls all around the court. If the ball hits a wall, a player **(33)** .... hit it again and so the game

continues for a lot longer. Like tennis, there is a net **(34)** .... the court and players hit a ball over it. Unlike tennis, the game is always doubles, never singles. It's longer, faster and very good **(35)** .... you!

26 **A** go   **B** do   **C** get   **D** seem

27 **A** all   **B** many   **C** whole   **D** every

28 **A** keep   **B** gain   **C** make   **D** continue

29 **A** more   **B** maximum   **C** majority   **D** most

30 **A** at   **B** in   **C** on   **D** to

31 **A** common   **B** exciting   **C** famous   **D** popular

32 **A** like   **B** same   **C** similar   **D** matching

33 **A** can   **B** ought   **C** shall   **D** would

34 **A** through   **B** across   **C** inside   **D** by

35 **A** at   **B** to   **C** for   **D** of

Tip strip

Question 26: Which of the verbs can also mean 'become'?

Question 27: 'Time' is singular and only one option fits without adding another word like 'of' or 'the'.

Question 30: Which preposition do we use with a country?

Question 32: You need a word that is followed by 'to'.

Question 33: Which modal shows 'possibility'?

Question 34: Which word means the same as 'from one side to the other'?

Question 35: Which word follows 'good' to mean 'it benefits'?

Writing: Parts 1–3

About the paper

Part 1
In Part 1, you read five pairs of sentences on the same topic, and complete a sentence transformation task. The pairs of sentences have the same meaning, but are expressed in different ways. You have to complete the second sentence so that it means the same as the first, using up to three words.

Part 2
In Part 2, you write a short communicative message, for example, a note, email or postcard. You must include the three points given in the instructions. You should write between 35 and 45 words.

Part 3
In Part 3, you must write one task from a choice of two. You can choose to write a letter or a story. For the letter, you are given part of a letter from an English-speaking friend and must write a reply. For the story, you are given either the title or the first line. You should write around 100 words.

How to do the paper

Part 1
- Look at the instructions and the example to get an idea of the topic.
- Read the first sentence and think about what it means. Then read the second and think about what is being tested, for example, active to passive form.
- Decide what is missing from the second sentence and write the missing words.
- Your answer may include words or expressions not used in the first sentence, but they should express the same idea. Don't include new details or change the original information.
- Make sure you haven't written more than three words. Remember that contracted words count as two words, for example, *won't = will not*.
- Check that the sentences make sense and that you have spelled the words correctly.

Part 2
- Don't be in a hurry to start writing. It's a good idea to spend a few minutes planning.

  Read the instructions carefully to understand:
  - who you are writing to and why
  - the three pieces of information you must include in your answer.
- Think about words and phrases you could use for each piece of information. Think about what tense you will use for each one.
- Write between 35 and 45 words. Remember to start with a greeting (for example, *Hi Anna*) and to add your name to sign off at the end.
- When you finish, check your writing. Have you included all three pieces of information? Have you made any basic mistakes that you can correct?

Part 3
- In Part 3, you can choose to write either a letter or a story. You should try to show the examiner the range of language and structures that you can use, so choose the task you are most confident about.

  Look carefully at each task and think about each one.
  - Are you confident you know how to write a letter to a friend? Do you know how to use the language you will need for the task (for example, describing something, giving advice)?
  - Look at the first line or title of the story. Do you have an idea for the story? Can you think of some interesting language you can use?
- **Letter**: Read the instructions carefully and underline the things you must include in your letter. Remember to: start and end appropriately (for example, *Hi Tom; All the best, Alex*), use informal language and be friendly throughout.
- **Story**: Make sure your story follows on from the first line, or is relevant to the title. Be careful if there are any names or pronouns in the title or first line and make sure your story continues with these. The story tests your ability to organise ideas into a beginning, middle and end, so pay attention to how you organise your writing and link ideas.
- Plan your answer, then write it using the appropriate format and style.
- When you have finished, check your writing. Have you included everything from the instructions? Have you used varied language? Are your points clearly expressed? Have you made any grammatical or spelling mistakes you can correct?

Writing: Part 1

Tip strip

Question 1: What is another way of saying that someone belongs to a club?

Question 2: Notice that the word 'teenager' is plural in the first sentence, but singular in the second. How can this help you?

Question 3: How can you change the sentence so that it is positive?

Question 4: How can we express a future possibility – think about a modal verb.

Question 5: Think about the subject of the second sentence and the word order when you have two objects of a verb.

Questions 1–5

Here are some sentences about a person who plays computer games.
For each question, complete the second sentence so that it means the same as the first.
Use no more than three words.
Write only the missing words.
In the exam, you write your answers **on a separate answer sheet.**
You may use this page for any rough work.

Example:

0   Bella started playing computer games five years ago.

  Bella .... **playing computer games for five years.**

0	*has been*

_____

1   She belongs to a big computer gaming club.

  She is .... **of a big computer gaming club.**

2   Bella is better than all the other teenagers in the club.

  Bella is .... **teenager in the club.**

3   Most games that people play aren't difficult enough for Bella.

  Most games that people play are .... **for Bella.**

4   It's possible that she will win an important competition next weekend.

  Bella .... **an important competition next weekend.**

5   Bella was given a new PC by her parents for her birthday last month.

  Bella's parents .... **a new PC for her birthday last month.**

Tip strip

Plan your answer before you start.

- Who are you going to write to?
- Why are you writing the email?
- What will you say first in your email?
- What did you like most about the holiday? Why? Which tense will you use?
- What phrase(s) can you use to suggest going on holiday together? Where could you go?

When you finish, check your answer for simple mistakes. Make sure you have written about all three points.

Question 6

You have just returned from a holiday.

Write an email to your English friend, Ben. In your email, you should:

- tell Ben where you went on holiday
- say what you enjoyed most about it
- suggest going on holiday together next year.

Write **35–45 words**.

In the exam, you write your answer **on a separate answer sheet**.

Tip strip

Which of these questions seems easier for you?

- Do you have enough ideas for the letter? Do you know the vocabulary you need? Remember you can invent some films if you can't think of any!

- Do you have an idea for the story? Do you know the vocabulary you need?

Try to include a good range of vocabulary and grammar in your answer.

Question 7: Write down some things you want to say in your letter. Try to deal with all the points that Olly mentions. How will you start and finish your letter?

Question 8: Think about what might happen next in the story. Why couldn't Charlie sleep? What did he do? Where did he go?

Write an answer to one of the questions (**7** or **8**) in this part.
Write your answer in about **100 words**.
In the exam, you write your answer **on a separate answer sheet**.
Mark the question number in the box at the top of your answer sheet.

Question 7

- This is part of a letter you receive from an English friend, Olly.

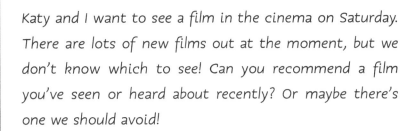

Katy and I want to see a film in the cinema on Saturday. There are lots of new films out at the moment, but we don't know which to see! Can you recommend a film you've seen or heard about recently? Or maybe there's one we should avoid!

- Now write a **letter** to Olly, answering his question.

Question 8

- Your English teacher has asked you to write a story.
- Your story must begin with this sentence:

Charlie couldn't sleep and got quietly out of bed.

- Now write your **story**.

Parts 1–4

About the paper

Paper 2 *Listening* takes about 30 minutes. There are four parts with a total of 25 questions. There is one mark for each answer. You will hear monologues and dialogues. You have time to read the questions before you listen to each part, and you will hear each recording twice.

Part 1
In Part 1, you listen to seven short extracts that are not connected to each other. They may be monologues or dialogues. There is one question along with three pictures for each extract. You have choose the correct picture to answer each question.

Part 2
In Part 2, you listen to a longer monologue or interview and answer six multiple-choice questions. There are three options to choose from for each question.

Part 3
In Part 3, you listen to a longer monologue. You are given a page of notes which summarise the information you hear. Six pieces of information are missing from the notes. You listen and complete the missing information, usually with one or two words or a number.

Part 4
In Part 4, you listen to a longer, informal dialogue. There are six statements for you to read. As you listen, you have to decide whether each statement is correct. If it is correct you answer 'yes' and if it is not correct you answer 'no'.

How to do the paper

Part 1
- Before you listen to each extract, read the question and look at the three pictures. This will prepare you for what you're going to hear.
- The first time you listen, try to understand the general meaning and think about the best answer. Remember you may hear all the options, but only one will answer the question.
- The second time you listen, check that your answer is correct.

Part 2
- Before you listen, read the instructions and all the questions. This will give you a general idea of what the listening text will be about.

  The questions come in the same order on the paper and in the listening text.
- Listen carefully. More than one of the options will be mentioned in the text, but only one of them will answer the question.
- The second time you listen, check that your answers are correct.

Part 3
- Before you listen, read the instructions and all the notes. Think about what type of information is missing. It may be one or two words, or a number.
- Listen the first time and fill in the information. If you don't hear the answer for one gap, don't worry. Leave it and carry on to the next.
- When you listen the second time, complete any information you missed and check your answers. Make sure you also check your spelling!

Part 4
- Before you listen, read the instructions and the six statements. Some statements are about whether the speakers agree or disagree with each other, so be ready to listen for this as well as for specific information.
- As you listen, choose A for 'yes' or B for 'no' for each statement. If you're not sure about one, don't worry. Move on to the next one.
- When you listen the second time, concentrate on any statements you weren't sure about and check your answers.

Part 1

Questions 1–7

There are seven questions in this part.
For each question, choose the correct answer (**A**, **B** or **C**).

Example: What is the boy going to buy with his birthday money?

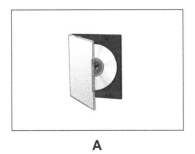

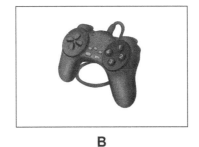

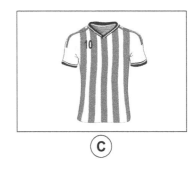

A   B   C

---

1   What will the girl do in the evening?

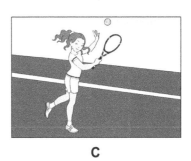

A   B   C

2   What did the boy like best about the geography lesson?

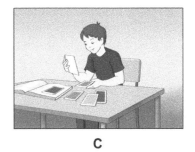

A   B   C

Tip strip
Question 1: Pay attention to the girl. She says what she intended to do before the boy called, then says what she will do now.

Question 2: The boy says he likes several things, but only one was the <u>most</u> fun.

3 When is the girl's next singing lesson?

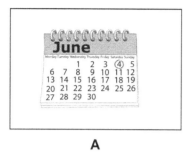

A

B

C

4 Which bag does the boy decide to use?

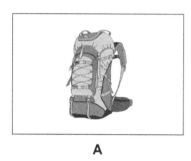

A

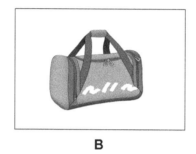

B

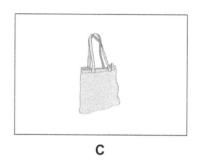

C

5 Where does Sarah live?

A

B

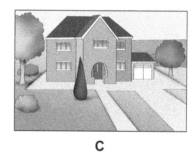

C

6   What musical instrument is the boy learning to play now?

A

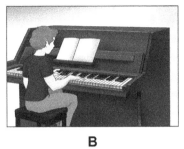

B

C

7   What does the girl want to do tomorrow?

A

B

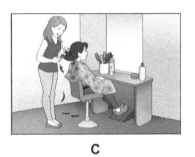

C

Tip strip

Question 8:
'Grandmother', 'friends' and 'mother' are all mentioned, but only one of them is the reason she started dancing.

Question 11: What does Sophie say is her 'favourite thing'?

Question 13: What does Sophie say she is 'sure' about? Which option has a word that means *sure*?

Part 2

Questions 8–13

You will hear an interview with a girl called Sophie Watson, who has just joined a professional dancing school.
For each question, choose the correct answer **A**, **B** or **C**.

8   Why did Sophie start dancing classes?

    A   Her grandmother suggested it.

    B   Her friends were already in the class.

    C   Her mother wanted her to try something new.

9   Why was Sophie's dad unhappy about her dancing?

    A   He thought she might get injured.

    B   He thought she wouldn't do her homework.

    C   He thought it was the wrong hobby.

10   Sophie felt nervous during her interview because

    A   she wanted to please her ballet teacher.

    B   she thought the other students were very good.

    C   she had to do a difficult dance.

11   What does Sophie enjoy most about daily life?

    A   Preparing for special performances.

    B   Training regularly.

    C   Learning with other dancers.

12   Sophie says that as a result of being at the school

    A   she has less time to relax.

    B   she has lost some of her friends.

    C   she has less fun than she did.

13   How does Sophie feel about her future?

    A   Certain she has made the correct choice.

    B   Confused about how good she is.

    C   Proud of being a big success.

Tip strip

Question 14: Make sure you listen for the <u>maximum</u> number of words.

Question 15: There are different numbers mentioned, but only one is the <u>minimum</u>.

Question 16: You hear different types of story, but only one is correct for the competition.

Questions 14–19

You will hear some information about a short-story competition.
For each question, fill in the missing information in the numbered space.

Short Story COMPETITION

Maximum length of story: **(14)** _____ words

Minimum number of characters: **(15)** _____

Type of story required: a **(16)** _____

Location of story: the **(17)** _____

Judges:

Jack Harris, author of a book called **(18)** '_____'

Carol Simmons, author and editor of 'Creative Writing' magazine.

Prizes:

First prize: a **(19)** _____

Other prizes: books and DVDs

Tip strip

Question 20: James has seen the film. Has Susie?

Question 22: Susie uses an expression for 'films of the past'. Does she like them or not?

Question 25: This question asks about whether the speakers agree or not. You have to listen very carefully to both of them. What word does James use before expressing his own opinion?

Questions 20–25

Look at the six sentences for this part.
You will hear a conversation between a girl, Susie, and a boy, James, about a new film called *One Evening*.
Decide if each sentence is correct or incorrect.
If it is correct, choose the letter **A** for **YES**. If it is not correct, choose the letter **B** for **NO**.

		YES	NO
20	Susie enjoyed watching the film *One Evening*.	A	B
21	James thinks the film uses special effects well.	A	B
22	Susie thinks acting in films was better in the past.	A	B
23	James prefers watching films in the cinema.	A	B
24	Susie often has a different opinion from film critics.	A	B
25	James disagrees with Susie about the future of cinema.	A	B

Parts 1–4

About the paper

The *Speaking* paper lasts 10–12 minutes. There are four parts, with a total of twenty-five marks. There are two candidates and two examiners. One examiner interacts with the candidates and the other acts as the assessor and just listens. Both candidates are marked on their individual performance throughout the whole test.

Part 1 (2–3 minutes)
In Part 1, the examiner asks you and your partner questions in turn. These questions are about everyday topics such as your personal interests, daily routines, likes and dislikes, etc.

Part 2 (2–3 minutes)
In Part 2, you and your partner are given instructions about something to discuss and reach a decision on, and a set of pictures to give you ideas. You have to give your opinion, listen to your partner's ideas and ask them about their opinions.

Part 3 (3 minutes)
In Part 3, you and your partner are each given a different colour photograph on the same topic. You have to talk about your own photograph for approximately one minute. You should describe what you can see in the photograph in as much detail as you can.

Part 4 (3 minutes)
In Part 4, the examiner asks you to discuss something related to the topic of the photographs in Part 3. You talk to your partner, giving your opinions on the topic, your personal experiences and your likes and dislikes. You also ask your partner for their ideas.

How to do the paper

Part 1
- Listen carefully to the examiner's questions and to your partner's answers. You might be asked the same or a similar question, or a completely different one.
- Give full answers, and include as much detail as you can.

Part 2
- Listen carefully to the examiner's instructions so that you understand the situation you have to talk about.
- Discuss each of the ideas illustrated in the pictures. Don't be afraid to give opinions and make comments about each one, agreeing or disagreeing with your partner.
- When you reach a decision, remember there are no right or wrong choices. You won't be given marks based on your opinions, but on the language you use.

Part 3
- Describe your photograph in as much detail as you can. You could include clothes, objects, the weather, what the people are doing, etc. Try to imagine you're describing the photograph to someone who can't see it. Remember to talk for around a minute.
- If you don't know or can't remember the name of an object in your photograph, don't worry – describe what it looks like and what it's used for.

Part 4
- Listen carefully to the task the examiner gives you.
- Cover the all points in as much detail as you can, and express your ideas clearly.
- Involve your partner in the discussion, by asking for his/her opinion and whether he/she agrees with you. Try to keep the discussion going for around three minutes, but the examiner can ask you extra questions to help you if necessary.

Part 1 (2–3 minutes)

Tip strip

Part 1

- Practise spelling your first name and surname so that you can do this easily in the exam.
- Be ready to talk about your studies and what you do in your spare time. Prepare useful vocabulary for these topics, but don't learn whole answers.
- Try to include as much detail as possible in your answers.

Phase 1

Good morning/afternoon/evening.

Can I have your mark sheets, please?

I'm … and this is ….

He/She is just going to listen to us.

Now, what's your name *(Candidate A)*?

Thank you.

And what's your name *(Candidate B)*?

Thank you.

Candidate B, what's your surname? How do you spell it?

Thank you

And Candidate A, what's your surname? How do you spell it?

Thank you.

Ask both candidates the following questions. Ask Candidate A first.
- Where do you live/come from?
- Do you study English at school?
- Do you like it?

Thank you.

Phase 2

Select one or more questions from the list to ask each candidate. Ask Candidate B first.
- How do you travel to school every day? Why?
- Tell us about your favourite teacher.
- Is there a subject at school you <u>don't</u> like? Why?
- Tell us about the house or flat where you live.

Thank you.

I'm going to describe a situation to you.

Some students in your class are going on a school **trip to the mountains** for the **weekend**. They can only take a **small bag** with them on the bus. Talk together about the **different** things they can put in their bag, then decide which would be **best**.

Here is a picture with some ideas to help you. [*Turn to the picture on page 51.*]

I'll say that again.

Some students in your class are going on a school **trip to the mountains** for the **weekend**. They can only take a **small bag** with them on the bus. Talk together about the **different** things they can put in their bag, then decide which would be **best**.

All right? Talk together.

Part 3 (3 minutes)

Now I'd like each of you to talk on your own about something. I'm going to give each of you a photograph of **people using mobile phones**.

Candidate A, here is your photograph. [*Look at Photograph 1A on page 52.*] Please show it to Candidate B, but I'd like you to talk about it. Candidate B, you just listen. I'll give you your photograph in a moment.

Candidate A, please tell us what you can see in your photograph.
(approximately 1 minute)

Thank you.

Now, Candidate B, here is your photograph. [*Look at Photograph 1B on page 53.*] It also shows **people using mobile phones**. Please show it to Candidate A and tell us what you can see in the photograph.
(approximately 1 minute)

Thank you.

Part 4 (3 minutes)

Your photographs showed **people using mobile phones**. Now, I'd like you to talk together about what **you** use **your mobile phone** for, and **places you don't like** to use it.

Thank you. That is the end of the test.

Practice Test 2

Reading: Part 1

Questions 1–5

Look at the text in each question. What does it say?
Choose the correct letter **A**, **B** or **C**.
In the exam, you mark your answers **on a separate answer sheet**.

Example:

0

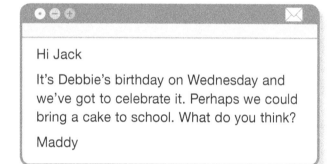

Hi Jack

It's Debbie's birthday on Wednesday and
we've got to celebrate it. Perhaps we could
bring a cake to school. What do you think?

Maddy

Why has Maddy written the email?

A To remind Jack about a birthday celebration.

B To ask Jack to buy something for the
celebration.

C To suggest a way to celebrate.

0	A	B	C
	⬜	⬜	▬

1

Guitar club

Wednesday's meeting
will be in Room 22, not Room 15
at same time.
Friday – back to normal.

What has changed?

A The day of the meeting.

B The time of the meeting.

C The place for the meeting

2

Bev,
Suzy called about Jane's party.
She wants your ideas about what
food to take. She's going to phone
again about 8.30 when she finishes
gym practice.

Why did Suzy phone?

A To tell Bev about her gym training.

B To ask Bev for some suggestions.

C To check the time of a party with Bev.

3

Brian

I've just put my name on the list for the London trip. Call me if you want me to add your name. Only three places left. It's £25 for the day. Tom's going too.

Olly

What should Brian do?

A Sign the list for a school trip.

B Pay Olly some money for the trip.

C Let Olly know if he wants to go on the trip.

4

Any laptops found
in classrooms will be taken
to the Head's office
for collection after school.

A If you find a laptop take it to your classroom teacher.

B If you can't find your laptop it might be in the Head's office.

C Students who leave laptops in classrooms will have to talk to the Head Teacher.

5

Jack,

Your swimming things are in your bag by the door. There are also some sandwiches to share with Kathy. She forgot to take hers earlier. Have a good swim!

Mum

What does Jack's mum want him to do?

A Take Kathy her swimming things.

B Give Kathy some food.

C Remind Kathy to go swimming.

Questions 6–10

The teenagers below all want to choose a TV programme to watch.
On the opposite page, there are descriptions of eight TV programmes.
Decide which programme would be most suitable for the following teenagers.
For questions **6–10**, choose the correct letter (**A–H**).
In the exam, you mark your answers **on a separate answer sheet**.

6

Ben enjoys seeing people compete in talent shows. He likes hearing new singers and also listening to the judges' comments. He usually guesses who is going to win.

7

Mandy is interested in drama, especially thrillers which continue over three or four days. That way she doesn't have to wait a week to see how it ends.

8

Alex wants to watch something which is true. He is particularly keen on learning about the working lives of famous people, especially actors and actresses.

9

Teresa loves playing the guitar and listening to music. She wants to watch a live concert with some of her favourite bands and maybe find a new singer to follow.

10

Carl reads about imaginary worlds and often goes to see films on the same subject. He'd like to watch a recent film, not an old classic because he's seen all those.

TV programmes

A You Heard it Here

This is a must for film fans. How much do you really know about what went on during the making of some of the most famous films ever? Michael Spencer interviews some of the biggest names in the film business and gets the real stories.

B Everyone's a Winner

It's that special time of year again when stars from film and TV receive awards for their achievements. The public have been voting for the last month and tonight we find out the results. There will also be awards for best TV music programme and the best song from a film. Last year, the song from the fantasy film *Night of the Dark Earth* won. Who will it be this evening?

C Carlton Crescent

This week on Carlton Crescent: we shall finally learn who caused the fire at the restaurant. The last few weeks have all been leading up to this thrilling episode. Did Fran really see a tall man in black start the blaze – or did she dream it? Don't miss it!

D At The Redland

Every year they face the mud and the rain to see some of the best music around today. If you can't be there, watch Channel 4's coverage of the final day of Redlandfest – as it happens – from the comfort of your living room. Famous names like the 'Cat Seekers' and new ones 'The Lost' will be on the main stage.

E Choices

John Tyler and Katy Napier discuss the week's best new films as usual at 4.30. Following this will be the TV premier of the film that won the Fantasy Prize at the Midlands Film Festival earlier this year. The judges made a good choice!

F The Chaser

There has been a lot of advertising for the exciting new three-part series *The Chaser* which starts tonight and finishes on Thursday. Kerry Watson, the writer, admits that it is based on a news item she read three years ago. But she insists that the character of the killer is imaginary!

G The Best

A new set of documentaries about famous twentieth-century writers starts this week. The first is about the life of Australian writer Jimmy Sutcliffe whose series about an Aborigine boy sold millions of copies. These programmes are both informative and memorable.

H Star

This week sees the last in the series of *Star*. We've followed their journeys from first auditions and watched them laugh and cry at the reactions they get. Tonight we find out who will win the top prize. Don't forget to phone in your vote, too.

Reading: Part 3

Questions 11–20

Look at the sentences below about a children's charity.
Read the text on the opposite page to decide if each sentence is correct or incorrect.
If it is correct, write **A**.
If it is not correct, write **B**.
In the exam, you mark your answers **on a separate answer sheet**.

---

11 The charity focuses on helping teenage children.

12 Children from various places and different families can have breaks at
Honeypot House.

13 These children require help because they have physical problems.

14 Because they are not able to take part in normal childhood activities they
do not always relate to other children well.

15 One benefit of a stay at Honeypot House is forming friendships with others
who have similar lives.

16 At Honeypot House children are taught skills that can help them when they
return home.

17 A special Play Bus transports the children to Honeypot House for their breaks.

18 When children visit the Play Buses that go to communities they are encouraged
to be creative.

19 The charity gets in touch with children they have helped at least twice a year.

20 Many people do not know about the work that these young carers do.

Honeypot House

Many people travel to the New Forest in the south of England for a holiday. They enjoy walking in the countryside and looking at the wild horses and trees. But this lovely area is also the home to a very famous children's charity – Honeypot House. It is the only children's charity in the UK that helps young children from five to twelve years old.

The children who are helped by Honeypot House are from different areas and different sorts of homes. They have one thing in common. They don't have a normal childhood. Many of these children are young carers who, from the age of five, have helped to look after adults in their families with medical problems. Perhaps a mother is disabled and the child needs to give her medicines and do some work around the house. These young children cannot have a normal childhood. They don't have the same hobbies, interests or do the same sports as other children. This means that it is often difficult for them to make friends at school. As a result they are also sometimes bullied.

Honeypot House allows these children to have short breaks in a beautiful environment where they can play and be free from the cares of their home lives. They meet other children who share their experiences and make good friends. The weekend breaks at Honeypot House offer the children lots of different activities. Among many other things, they can swim, ride bikes and play with animals. Most importantly, they can have fun and have amazing memories to help them through their difficult lives.

Not all young carers can have the opportunity to stay at Honeypot House. There aren't enough places. So, the charity has a special Play Bus which visits children in the community. It travels to many areas. The Bus is equipped with toys and games, and the children who play on the Bus can do a variety of things such as art, dance and music. Again, very importantly, they meet other children in their area who are in similar situations.

Once you become a Honeypot Child you are not forgotten. The charity sends birthday and Christmas cards and every year it goes round the country to give out Christmas presents to its children. These young carers are often forgotten by society because what they do isn't seen or recognised by others. But they need to have a chance to enjoy their childhood and Honeypot House tries to do that for at least some of them.

Questions 21–25

Read the text and questions below.
For each question, choose the correct letter **A**, **B**, **C** or **D**.
In the exam, you mark your answers **on a separate answer sheet**.

Local Teenager of the Year

This year's awards took place last night in Merton Town Hall. Every year, local people vote for a teenager who has managed to live with a particular problem and this year's winner was Laura Parker. When people look at Laura they see a happy teenager, but her life has been difficult. Laura has been deaf since birth. Her parents have always encouraged her to get the most out of life in spite of her disability. When Laura's parents realised very early on that their daughter had severe hearing problems they were determined not to let it affect her life too badly. They didn't treat her any differently from her brother and sister, and always let her do the same activities as they did.

Of course, they had to help her communicate and she started to learn sign language as early as possible.

'We obviously had to learn it as well,' says her mother Karen and laughs. 'It was really hard – but extremely interesting!' Now Laura is an expert at 'signing' and 'lip-reading', too, and it's her main way of talking to people. She wears very strong hearing aids which can give her some sounds. Her parents hope that when she is older she will be able to have a special operation to put a small electronic device inside her head behind her ear that will receive sounds better. In the meantime, Laura manages her life and has a wide circle of friends at school and at her gymnastics club.

Recently, Laura got a wonderful present – a hearing dog called Lucy. Lucy has been specially trained to help people who are deaf. She gives a signal to Laura if her phone rings or if someone knocks at the door. She runs up to her and then runs to the phone or the door. She does the same thing if someone calls Laura's name.

So, our congratulations go to Laura for her award. If you know about a teenager you'd like to suggest for next year's award tell us about him or her on our website.

21 What is the writer's main purpose in writing the text?

   A   To give advice to deaf people.
   B   To describe the life of a deaf person.
   C   To praise someone who has helped deaf people.
   D   To encourage readers to attend an event for deaf people.

22 When Laura was young her parents

   A   worried that she wasn't the same as other people.
   B   wanted her to enjoy life as much as possible.
   C   selected the things she could do carefully.
   D   were optimistic about her future.

23 How does Laura understand and speak to people?

   A   A small device put in her head allows her to hear a little.
   B   Her parents know what she wants to say and communicate for her.
   C   She relies on hearing aids all the time.
   D   She uses a special form of communication with lips and hands.

24 Laura's dog Lucy is able to

   A   open the door when people knock.
   B   understand when people call her name.
   C   make Laura aware of certain sounds.
   D   help people train other dogs.

25 What might Laura say about her life?

   A
   I didn't really enjoy my life much when I was young, but now Lucy makes me very happy.

   B
   I love signing because my parents can't understand me and I can have fun, but it will be good to hear properly.

   C
   Life isn't always easy but I can do nearly everything that I want to and I've got lots of friends and interests.

   D
   People sometimes treat me differently because I have a disability and I don't like that at all and it can make me angry.

Questions 26–35

Read the text below and choose the correct word for each space.
For each question, choose the correct letter **A**, **B**, **C** or **D**.
In the exam, you mark your answers **on a separate answer sheet**.

Example:

0   **A**   since   **B**   until   **C**   from   **D**   for

0	A	B	C	D

No gum!

We've been buying chewing gum **(0)** .... over a hundred and fifty years and today it is **(26)** .... popular than ever. **(27)** ...., it causes a lot of problems, particularly in the streets. People **(28)** .... their gum on pavements and it sticks hard, like stone. This **(29)** .... that it is very difficult to clean up. Cities and towns spend a lot of money on special equipment to try to get it **(30)** .... the pavements. It can **(31)** .... a city about £20,000 for one cleaning session!

An environmental group in London is trying to make people more aware of the problem in a clever **(32)** .... They use special **(33)** .... yellow paint to put a circle around each piece of gum on the pavement. They hope people **(34)** .... change their habits and put their chewing gum in the bin. They need to. In one year the chewing gum from two main streets **(35)** .... London would cover twelve football pitches!

26 **A** very   **B** most   **C** much   **D** more

27 **A** Despite   **B** However   **C** As well   **D** Although

28 **A** drop   **B** let   **C** put   **D** fall

29 **A** means   **B** finds   **C** makes   **D** stays

30 **A** out   **B** up   **C** off   **D** over

31 **A** cost   **B** pay   **C** spend   **D** buy

32 **A** path   **B** direction   **C** way   **D** task

33 **A** big   **B** clear   **C** happy   **D** bright

34 **A** to   **B** will   **C** must   **D** going

35 **A** at   **B** in   **C** on   **D** by

Questions 1–5

Here are some sentences about a person who has recently moved house.
For each question, complete the second sentence so that it means the same
as the first.
Use no more than three words.
Write only the missing words.
In the exam, you write your answers **on a separate answer sheet**.
You may use this page for any rough work.

Example:

0   Before his family moved to London, Peter's home was in a small village.

Before his family moved to London, Peter .... **live
in a small village.**

0	*used to*

---

1   Now Peter goes to a smaller school than before.

Peter's new school isn't .... **his last one.**

2   He doesn't live very near his new school.

He lives quite a .... **from his new school.**

3   If he gets the 7.30 bus he can get to school on time.

He can't get to school on time .... **he gets
the 7.30 bus.**

4   He usually visits his old friends every two weeks.

He usually visits his old friends .... **a month.**

5   Peter would rather live in the village than in London.

Peter would prefer .... **in the village than
in London.**

Question 6

You have just been to a concert.

Write an email to your English friend, Mark. In your email, you should:

- tell Mark what concert you went to
- say what you liked most about it
- ask about the music Mark likes.

Write **35–45 words**.

In the exam, you mark your answers **on a separate answer sheet**.

Writing: Part 3

Write an answer to one of the questions (**7** or **8**) in this part.
Write your answer in about **100 words**.
In the exam, you mark your answers **on a separate answer sheet**.
Mark the question number in the box at the top of your answer sheet.

Question 7

- This is part of an email you receive from an English friend, Carl.

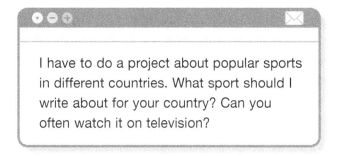

I have to do a project about popular sports in different countries. What sport should I write about for your country? Can you often watch it on television?

- Now write an **email** to Carl, answering his question.

Question 8

- Your English teacher has asked you to write a story.
- Your story must begin with this sentence:

The train stopped again and Beth looked at her watch.

- Now write your **story**.

Questions 1–7

There are seven questions in this part.
For each question, choose the correct answer (**A**, **B** or **C**).

Example: What is the boy going to buy with his birthday money?

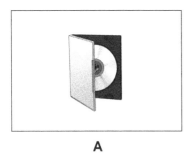 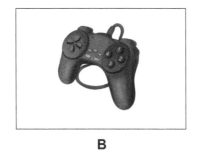 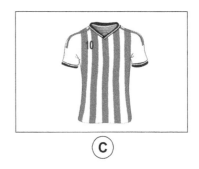

A   B   (C)

---

1 What does the boy decide to take to school for lunch?

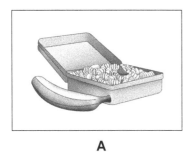 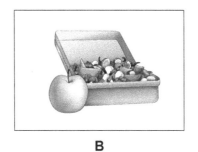 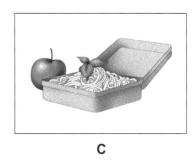

A   B   C

2 What did the girl like best about her holiday?

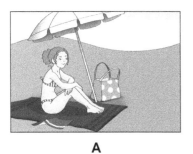  

A   B   C

3 Which photograph is the boy's cousin?

  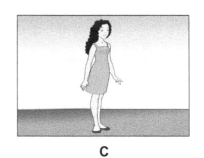

A   B   C

4 Which TV programme does the girl agree to watch?

A

B

C

5 What will the weather be like on Saturday?

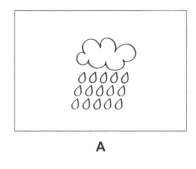

A

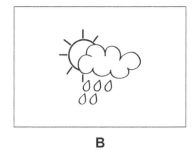

B

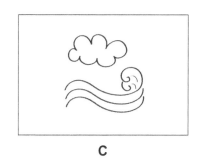

C

6 Where is the boy's homework book?

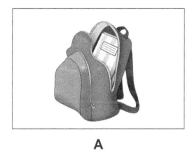

A

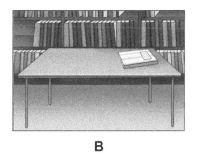

B

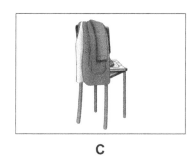

C

7 What is the girl waiting for?

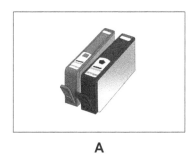

A

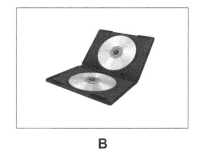

B

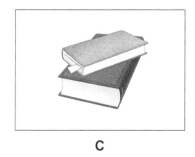

C

Part 2

Questions 8–13

You will hear an interview with a boy called Jack Roberts, who has become famous as a singer in his own country at the age of twelve.
For each question, choose the correct answer **A**, **B** or **C**.

---

8 How did Jack's career as a singer start?

    A He won a competition.

    B He sang on television.

    C He performed in different live events.

9 When Jack is on stage he is

    A afraid he won't perform well.

    B happy that people like his performance.

    C keen to sing new songs.

10 Jack is embarrassed when he sees himself on film because

    A he doesn't do enough practice.

    B he always makes too many mistakes.

    C he knows his performance is not perfect.

11 What does Jack find most difficult about being famous?

    A Having to travel a lot.

    B Missing his family.

    C Meeting fans everywhere.

12 How does Jack feel about doing schoolwork?

    A He doesn't like doing it alone.

    B He doesn't have time to do it all.

    C He doesn't think it's useful for his future.

13 Jack says his next music album

    A will be different from his first one.

    B will be based on personal experience.

    C wlll be written for a different age group.

Questions 14–19

You will hear some information about visiting a space museum.
For each question, fill in the missing information in the numbered space.

Space museum

Entry

Saturday and Sunday: open until: **(14)** _____

Closed on: **(15)** _____ and bank holidays

Advance tickets: **(16)** £ _____ for family of four

Exhibitions and activities

Films every hour: 'Beyond the Moon'

(17) ' _____ '

In the Blue Room: **(18)** _____ to use

Competition prizes: books and DVDs

Lecturers

Mary Jones, scientist

Dan Richards, author of **(19)** ' _____ '

Food and drink

Café on top floor

Part 4

Questions 20–25

Look at the six sentences for this part.
You will hear a conversation between a girl, Alice, and a boy, Oliver, about spending a month
at a summer camp during their school holiday.
Decide if each sentence is correct or incorrect.
If it is correct, choose the letter **A** for **YES**. If it is not correct, choose the letter **B** for **NO**.

		YES	NO
20	Oliver was surprised at how popular the summer camp was.	A	B
21	Alice found it easy to make new friends.	A	B
22	Oliver didn't enjoy being away from his family.	A	B
23	Alice thinks Oliver should have done more sports.	A	B
24	Oliver learned a new skill at the summer camp.	A	B
25	Alice agrees with her parents about going to summer camp.	A	B

Part 1 (2–3 minutes)

Phase 1

Good morning/afternoon/evening.

Can I have your mark sheets, please?

I'm … and this is …

He/she is just going to listen to us.

Now, what's your name *(Candidate A)*?

Thank you.

And what's your name *(Candidate B)*?

Thank you.

Candidate B, what's your surname? How do you spell it?

Thank you.

And Candidate A, what's your surname? How do you spell it?

Thank you.

Ask both candidates the following questions. Ask Candidate A first.
- Where do you live/come from?
- Do you study English at school?
- Do you like it?

Thank you.

Phase 2

Select one or more questions from the list to ask each candidate. Ask Candidate B first.
- Tell us about your family.
- What's your favourite subject at school? Why?
- What would you like to do when you are older? Why?
- Tell us about the school day.

Thank you.

Part 2 (2–3 minutes)

I'm going to describe a situation to you.

There are two **new** students in a class. The **other students** in the class want to **do something** to make them **feel welcome**. Talk together about the **different** things the other students could do and then decide which would be **best**.

Here is a picture with some ideas to help you. [*Turn to the picture on page 54.*]

I'll say that again.

There are two **new** students in a class. The **other students** in the class want to **do something** to make them **feel welcome**. Talk together about the **different** things the other students could do and then decide which would be **best**.

All right? Talk together.

Part 3 (3 minutes)

Now I'd like each of you to talk on your own about something. I'm going to give each of you a photograph of **friends spending an afternoon together**.

Candidate A, here is your photograph. [*Look at Photograph 2A on page 55.*] Please show it to Candidate B, but I'd like you to talk about it. Candidate B, you just listen. I'll give you your photograph in a moment.

Candidate A, please tell us what you can see in the photograph.
(approximately 1 minute)

Thank you.

Now, Candidate B, here is your photograph. [*Look at Photograph 2B on page 56.*] It also shows **friends spending an afternoon together**. Please show it to Candidate A and tell us what you can see in the photograph.
(approximately 1 minute)

Thank you.

Part 4 (3 minutes)

Your photographs showed **friends spending an afternoon together**. Now I'd like you to talk together about the things **you** like to do with **your friends after school**, and the things **you** like to do with **your friends at the weekends**.

Thank you. That is the end of the test.

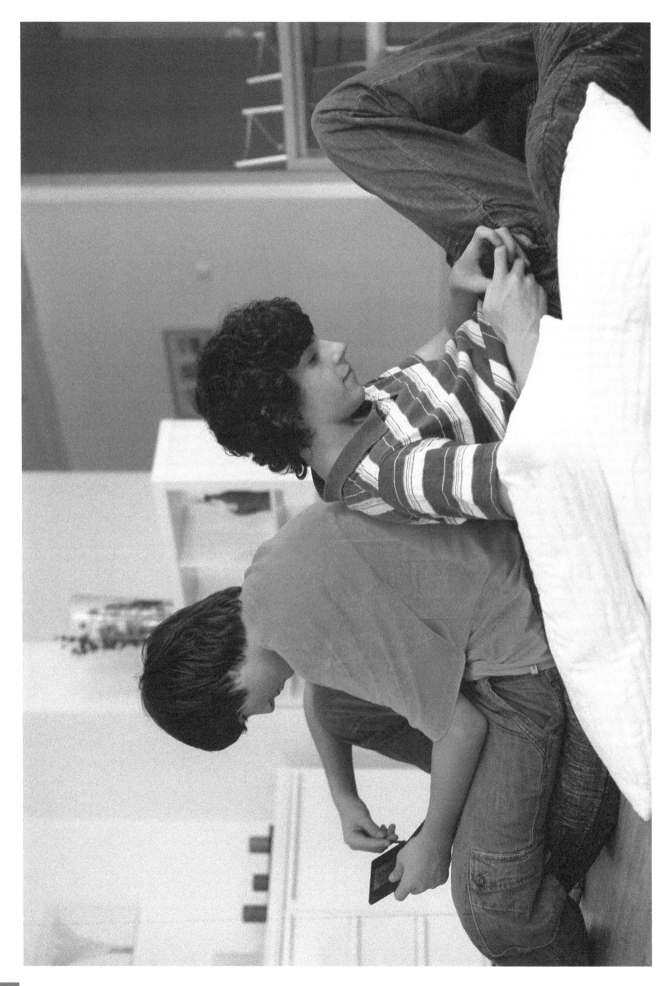

Writing Bank

Part 2: Short message

You have just returned from a holiday.

Write an email to your English friend, Ben. In your email you should:

*   tell Ben where you went on holiday
*   say what you enjoyed most about it
*   suggest going on holiday next year.

Write **35–45 words**. In the exam, you write your answer **on a separate answer sheet**.

Example answer

this is the first content point

this is the third content point

use a closing expression

Hi Ben,

I'm back from holiday. We went to Spain and stayed in a great hotel. I met some very nice people and I'm going to write to them all. Why don't we go camping together next year in my country? That would be fun!

Write soon

David

use first names

this is the second content point

use informal punctuation such as exclamation marks

use lively language to add interest

*   Read the instructions very carefully.
*   Make sure you include all the content points.
*   Address your email to the right person.
*   Check how many words you have used.
*   Try to include some interesting vocabulary.
*   Include a suitable closing.
*   Check your grammar for mistakes.

Thanking
I want to thank you for …
Thank you so much for …
I really enjoyed …

Apologising
I'm really sorry, but …
I'm so sorry I can't …
I'm very sorry about …

Suggesting and recommending
I think the best thing is to …
Why don't you … ?
Let's …
You should …
If I were you, I would …

Reminding
You must remember to …
Please don't forget to …
Remember you have to …….

Inviting
I hope you can …
Would you like to … ?

Explaining
I can't come because I have to …
I like it because …
I don't want to do it because …

Practice Activity: **Checking your work**

Correct 8 mistakes in the short note below. Think about grammar and spelling.

Hi Jo,
I realy enjoied spending a week at you home – I had the great time. The best part is going to that football match – I've never saw such an amazing stadium! I'm look forward to next year when you will visiting my home.
Love,
Sue

Part 3: Informal letter

- This is part of a letter you receive from an English friend, Olly.

> Katy and I want to see a film in the cinema on Saturday. There are lots of new films out at the moment but we don't know which to see! Can you recommend a film you've seen or heard about recently? Or maybe there's one we should avoid!

- Now write a **letter** to Olly, answering his question.
- Use **about 100** words.

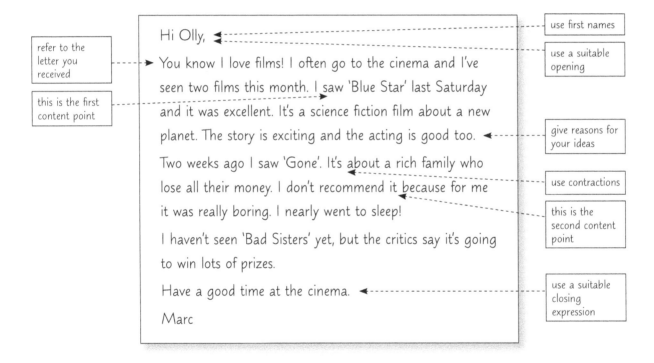

refer to the letter you received	use first names
this is the first content point	use a suitable opening

Hi Olly,

You know I love films! I often go to the cinema and I've seen two films this month. I saw 'Blue Star' last Saturday and it was excellent. It's a science fiction film about a new planet. The story is exciting and the acting is good too.

Two weeks ago I saw 'Gone'. It's about a rich family who lose all their money. I don't recommend it because for me it was really boring. I nearly went to sleep!

I haven't seen 'Bad Sisters' yet, but the critics say it's going to win lots of prizes.

Have a good time at the cinema.

Marc

give reasons for your ideas

use contractions

this is the second content point

use a suitable closing expression

- Read the instructions very carefully.
- Address your letter to the right person.
- Write your letter in a suitable style.
- Use paragraphs to divide the letter into clear sections.
- Try to include interesting vocabulary to make your letter lively.

- Using linking words to join your letter together.
- Count the number of words you have used.
- Try to avoid making spelling mistakes.
- Make sure you have included all the content points.

Useful language

Starting a letter/email

Dear/Hi James

Thanks for your letter/email.

I hope you're well.

It was great to hear from you!

Giving advice/making suggestions

If I were you …

Why don't we/you … ?

I suggest …

I think we/you should …

You could always …

Asking for/giving information

Could you tell me about …

Let me tell you about …

I need to know about …

You need to know that …

Saying what you think

In my opinion, …

It seems to me that …

I think that …

Ending a letter/email

Best wishes

Write soon

See you

Speak soon

Love

Practice Activity: Doing everything in the task

Choose the correct option for each sentence.

1 Why don't we see a film tonight?
(suggesting / accepting an invitation)

2 I'm afraid I'm going to be late.
(apologising / explaining)

3 Thanks for meeting me.
(offering / thanking)

4 My house is quite big, with a large garden.
(describing / giving directions)

5 I'll give it back to you tomorrow.
(offering / promising)

6 I'd love to visit you next year.
(accepting an invitation / making an offer)

7 OK – I'll come to your house instead.
(disagreeing / making a decision)

8 What would you like to do in the evening?
(asking for information / asking for help)

Part 3: Story

Example question

- Your English teacher has asked you to write a story.
- Your story must begin with this sentence:

Charlie couldn't sleep and got quietly out of bed.

Now write your **story**. Use **about 100** words.

Example answer

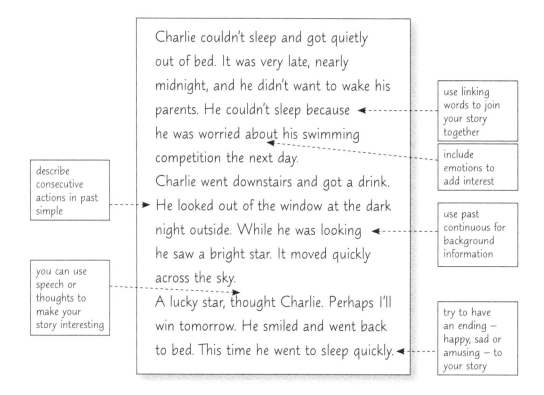

describe consecutive actions in past simple

you can use speech or thoughts to make your story interesting

Charlie couldn't sleep and got quietly out of bed. It was very late, nearly midnight, and he didn't want to wake his parents. He couldn't sleep because he was worried about his swimming competition the next day.
Charlie went downstairs and got a drink. He looked out of the window at the dark night outside. While he was looking he saw a bright star. It moved quickly across the sky.
A lucky star, thought Charlie. Perhaps I'll win tomorrow. He smiled and went back to bed. This time he went to sleep quickly.

use linking words to join your story together

include emotions to add interest

use past continuous for background information

try to have an ending – happy, sad or amusing – to your story

Exam help

- Read the instructions very carefully.
- If you are given a sentence to use in the story, do not change it.
- Use the names or places that you are given.
- Make sure you write about the right number of words.
- Divide your story into clear sections with paragraphs.
- Use a range of vocabulary and phrases to add interest to your story.
- Check your grammar, particularly verb tenses, carefully.

Useful language

Adding interest
At that exact moment, …
Completely unexpectedly, …
Suddenly, I realised that …
All at once …

Saying exactly when things happened
It all started when …
Later, …
At the same time, …
After that, …
By now …

Using adjectives/adverbs for interest
It was a **wonderful/terrible** film.
She felt **completely happy**.
It was a **great** party.
I was **rather bored**.
I was **absolutely terrified**.
I ran **quickly** to the door.

Ending a story
It was the best day of my life.
Suddenly, I woke up.
Then I realised it was over.
I felt totally happy.
I didn't want it to end.

Practice Activity: Making a story easy to understand

Fill in the gaps in the story using phrases from the box.

after that   any   long   rather   suddenly   unexpectedly

A boring day

I had nothing to do and all my friends had gone to the beach for the day, so I was **(1)** ……………………… bored. I didn't have **(2)** ……………………… money left, so I couldn't go shopping. I decided to finish my homework. **(3)** ……………………… there was a knock on the door. It was an old friend who had moved to a different school two years ago. We sat and talked for a **(4)** ……………………… . time. Then, completely **(5)** ……………………… , she said she was moving back to my school next semester. **(6)** ……………………… , we made lots of plans for things to do together!

Practice Activity: Making a story interesting

Choose the best word(s) to complete the story.

A terrible fright

It was a dark and windy night. **(1)** *Completely unexpectedly / First*, I heard a loud noise. I **(2)** *walked / ran quickly* downstairs and opened the front door. I looked all round, but couldn't see anyone. I went back inside. **(3)** *All at once / So* the noise came again. I **(4)** *hurried / went* to the door again, but I could see nothing. **(5)** *Then / By now* I was feeling **(6)** *absolutely / a little* terrified, so I called my friend. She came to my house, and we sat in the living room, waiting. The noise came again. We **(7)** *looked / stared* outside – and saw that a tree was blowing in the **(8)** *heavy / strong* wind and hitting the downstairs window. I felt extremely stupid!

Speaking Bank

Part 1: Giving personal information

Introducing yourself

My name's Alexandre Petrovitch, but my friends call me Alex.

Giving personal information

I've got (an older brother) and (two younger sisters).

I live in …

I'm studying …

I go to school in …

I get up (quite early) every morning.

I go out with my friends after school/at the weekend.

In my free time, I …

My favourite subject at school is …

I don't like studying … because …

My favourite teacher is … because …

If you don't understand/hear

Could you say that again, please?

Sorry, I didn't understand that. Could you repeat it, please?

Pardon?

What do you mean?

Practice Activity: About myself

Complete the sentences below, giving information about yourself.

1 My name's …
2 I live in …
3 I like learning English because …
4 My favourite school subject is … because …
5 After school, I usually …
6 In the mornings, I always …
7 At the weekend, I often …
8 My best friend is …
9 Yesterday I … with my friends.
10 My favourite television programme is …
11 I don't like studying … because …
12 I like going on holiday to … because …
13 My favourite food is … because …
14 I enjoy … with my family because …
15 The job I want to do in the future is … because …

Part 2: Discussing a situation

Asking for and making suggestions

What about (going swimming)?

We could try (walking).

I think (mountain biking) would be a good idea.

What do you think about … ?

What do you think we should do?

Have you got any ideas?

Giving, explaining and asking for opinions

I think (a book) is the best present because it's small.

In my opinion, giving her flowers is a good idea. She loves them.

I think we should buy her a pen because she always forgets hers.

What about you?

What do you think?

Do you think … would be a good idea?

Do you agree with me?

That's not a good idea, because (it's too big to carry).

Agreeing

I really agree with you.

That's a good idea.

That's true/right.

That's a good point.

Definitely!

That's just what I think.

Exactly!

Disagreeing

Maybe that's not such a good idea.

I don't think so.

I can't completely agree with that.

Perhaps you're right, but …

I'm not sure about that.

I don't think that's right.

Making decisions

Let's choose …

Why don't we decide on … ?

That's the best one.

So what shall we choose?

So we both think this is the best one.

Part 3: Describing a photograph

Identifying parts of the picture

In the top/bottom right/left-hand corner

Saying where people are

They're standing near the window.

They're sitting on a sofa.

They're walking along the beach/in a town.

Behind the man there's a boy.

There's a girl standing in front of the restaurant.

Describing people

The girl's quite short/tall.

The boy's got dark/fair/hair.

He's wearing blue jeans and a red scarf.

She's wearing sunglasses and a cap.

Describing places

The town looks rather crowded.

It seems to be a busy market.

The park looks beautiful.

It looks sunny/windy/cold.

The mountains are beautiful.

Making guesses

I think they look quite happy.

They seem a bit bored/tired.

It looks as if they're having fun/problems.

I don't know what this is, but I think it's a …

Maybe they're friends.

They might be enjoying the situation.

When you don't know the word for something

I don't know what this is in English, but you take photographs with it.

It's like an orange.

You wear it round your neck.

Practice Activity: **Giving/asking for opinions**

Put a question mark at the end of the sentences that are asking for an opinion.

1   Do you have any ideas
2   What I think is this
3   How about you
4   In my opinion it's great
5   How do you feel about that
6   That's not what I think
7   What do you think
8   What would you say
9   This seems to be good
10 Do you think the same as me
11 It seems to me to be a bad idea
12 I suppose it could be useful

Practice Activity: **Responding to others**

Look at the dialogues 1–10. What is B doing? Choose from the box below.

A adding information	F disagreeing
B agreeing	G explaining
C asking for an opinion	H giving an opinion
D asking for more information	I making a decision
E changing the topic	J making a suggestion

1   A   I think sport on television is boring.
    B   Really? Why do you say that?   …
2   A   I think playing tennis would be fun.
    B   That's not a very good idea.   …
3   A   I think we should give her flowers.
    B   I don't know. What about chocolates?   …
4   A   What about going swimming tomorrow?
    B   I'm not sure – what do you think about it?   …
5   A   We should talk about this one first.
    B   You're right – let's start now.   …
6   A   Can you tell me what this picture is?
    B   Yes – it's a café. There are people eating.   …
7   A   Which present shall we get? The camera?
    B   I think so – yes – we'll choose that.   …
8   A   Going to a restaurant seems like a good idea to me.
    B   We've already talked about that. Let's talk about the cinema instead.   …
9   A   I think the film was great.
    B   Yes, there was so much action – it was very exciting.   …
10 A   What do you think about giving these flowers as a present?
    B   What I think is that they're rather expensive. …

Practice Activity: Talking about a photograph

1 Look at the photograph and read what a student said about it. Choose the best alternatives to complete the text.

I can see two girls and I think they are friends. They are using their mobile phone to take a photograph of **(1)** *themselves / ourselves*. Perhaps they are having a day out together and they want to remember it. They are sitting **(2)** *outside / inside* at a table. Maybe they are at a **(3)** *café / restaurant* because there are some flowers behind them. They are both holding a **(4)** *glass / cup* with a drink in it – **(5)** *then / perhaps* it is coffee or some other drink. The girl on the **(6)** *right / left* is holding the camera, so she is taking the photograph. She is wearing a grey **(7)** *blouse / jacket* and she has **(8)** *dark / fair* hair. The girl next to her is wearing a blue jacket, and she has **(9)** *short / long* red hair. I think they are enjoying their day **(10)** *so / because* they are both smiling and they look happy.

2 Look at the photograph and read what a student said about it. Choose the best alternatives to complete the text.

I can see two boys. Maybe they're friends, or they could be brothers. They are sitting on **(1)** *pillows / cushions* on the floor, and they are both using their mobile phones. Perhaps they are texting or **(2)** *anything / something* like that. They are not talking together and they have their **(3)** *backs / fronts* to each **(4)** *other / another*. The boy on the **(5)** *left / right* is wearing an orange T-shirt and blue jeans, and he has short dark hair. The boy on the right is also wearing jeans but he has a **(6)** *plain / striped* T-shirt and has dark **(7)** *straight / curly* hair. Behind them I can see white shelves and a **(8)** *cup / vase* of flowers, so I think they are in their **(9)** *living room / bedroom*. They both look happy, so they are probably relaxing **(10)** *after / at* school and contacting their friends by text.

Part 4: Having a discussion

If you're not sure what to say

That's a difficult question.
Well, I suppose that …
I'm not really sure about that, but possibly …
I haven't thought about that before, but …
Let me think …

Explaining likes and dislikes

Do you like playing tennis? Not really, because …
I enjoy watching …
I'm not keen on …
My favourite kind of music/food is …
I'd rather live in … than … because …
I like …, but I prefer …
What I like best about school is …
I'd rather go to the cinema than the theatre

Listening and responding to your partner

You said you often … and that's very interesting.
I know you like … and I do, too.
You said you don't like …, but I do.
You live in …, but I've never been there. What's it like?

Practice Activity: Responding to your partner

Match the responses A–J to the sentences (1–10).

1 I didn't understand what you said.   …
2 Shall I start?   …
3 Let's go back and talk about music again.   …
4 Do you agree with me?   …
5 Excuse me – can I say something?   …
6 What do you mean?   …
7 I really love watching films on TV at home. …
8 At the weekend I often play tennis with my Dad. …
9 You said you don't like swimming, but I do. …
10 You live in Paris, but I've never been there. …

A Well, what I mean is that it would be fun.
B Good idea – we didn't finish talking about it.
C OK – I'll put it another way.
D Certainly – go ahead.
E I do that after school. At the weekend we swim.
F Oh, I'm sorry – please say what you think.
G Actually, I'm sorry but I don't really agree.
H Do you? I prefer watching them in the cinema.
I You must go – it's a really beautiful place.
J Really? I hate getting wet!